GOD THE SAVIOR

A Gospel-Centered Exploration in
NUMBERS and JOSHUA

PHILIP NATION & ROBERT SMITH

LifeWay Press®
Nashville, Tennessee

Item: 006102094
ISBN: 978-1-4300-5443-6
Dewey decimal classification number: 234
Subject heading: OBEDIENCE / GOD / FAITH

Eric Geiger
Vice President, LifeWay Resources

Ed Stetzer
General Editor

Trevin Wax
Managing Editor

Michael Kelley
Director, Groups Ministry

Joel Polk
Content Editor

We believe that the Bible has God for its author; salvation for its end; and truth, without any mixture of error, for its matter and that all Scripture is totally true and trustworthy. To review LifeWay's doctrinal guideline, please visit *lifeway.com/doctrinalguideline*.

Unless otherwise noted, all Scripture quotations are taken from the Holman Christian Standard Bible®, copyright 1999, 2000, 2002, 2003, 2009 by Holman Bible Publishers. Used by permission. Scripture quotations marked ESV are from The Holy Bible, English Standard Version® (ESV®), copyright © 2001 by Crossway, a publishing ministry of Good News Publishers. Used by permission. All rights reserved.

For ordering or inquiries, visit *lifeway.com;* write LifeWay Small Groups; One LifeWay Plaza; Nashville, TN 37234-0152; or call toll free (800) 458-2772.

Printed in the United States of America.

Groups Ministry Publishing
LifeWay Resources
One LifeWay Plaza
Nashville, Tennessee 37234-0152

TABLE OF CONTENTS

ABOUT THE GOSPEL PROJECT

Some people see the Bible as a collection of stories with morals for life application. But it's so much more. Sure, the Bible has some stories in it, but it's also full of poetry, history, codes of law and civilization, songs, prophecy, letters—even a love letter. When you tie it all together, something remarkable happens. A story is revealed. One story. The story of redemption through Jesus. This is *The Gospel Project.*

When we begin to see the Bible as the story of redemption through Jesus Christ, God's plan to rescue the world from sin and death, our perspective changes. We no longer look primarily for what the Bible says about us but instead see what it tells us about God and what He has done. After all, it's the gospel that saves us, and when we encounter Jesus in the pages of Scripture, the gospel works on us, transforming us into His image. *We become God's gospel project.*

ABOUT THE WRITERS

Philip Nation (sessions 1-2) is the content development director for LifeWay and the teaching pastor for The Fellowship, a multi-campus church in Nashville, Tennessee. His newest book is *Habits for Our Holiness: How the Spiritual Disciplines Grow Us Up, Draw Us Together, and Send Us Out.*

Robert Smith (sessions 3-6) is a professor of Christian preaching and holds the Charles T. Carter Baptist Chair of Divinity at Beeson Divinity School in Birmingham, Alabama. He is the author of *Doctrine That Dances.* He is married to Dr. Wanda Taylor-Smith, and they have four adult children with one in heaven.

Alicia Claxon adapted this material for use with small groups.

HOW TO USE THIS STUDY

Welcome to *The Gospel Project*, a gospel-centered small-group study that dives deep into the things of God, lifts up Jesus, focuses on the grand story of Scripture, and drives participants to be on mission. This small-group Bible study provides opportunities to study the Bible and to encounter the living Christ. *The Gospel Project* provides you with tools and resources to purposefully study God's Word and to grow in the faith and knowledge of God's Son. And what's more, you can do so in the company of others, encouraging and building up one another. Here are some things to remember that will help you maximize the usefulness of this resource:

GATHER A GROUP. We grow in the faith best in community with other believers, as we love, encourage, correct, and challenge one another. The life of a disciple of Christ was never meant to be lived alone, in isolation.

PRAY. Pray regularly for your group members.

PREPARE. This resource includes the Bible study content, three devotionals, and discussion questions for each session. Work through the session and devotionals in preparation for each group session. Take notes and record your own questions. Also consider the follow-up questions so you are ready to participate in and add to the discussion, bringing up your own notes and questions where appropriate.

RESOURCE YOURSELF. Make good use of the additional resources available on the Web at *gospelproject.com/additionalresources* and search for this specific title. Download a podcast. Read a blog post. Be intentional about learning from others in the faith. For tips on how to better lead groups or additional ideas for leading this Bible study, visit: *ministrygrid.com/web/thegospelproject*.

GROUP TIME. Gather together with your group to discuss the session and devotional content. Work through the follow-up questions and your own questions. Discuss the material and the implications for the lives of believers and the mission to which we have been called.

OVERFLOW. Remember…*The Gospel Project* is not just a Bible study. *We* are the project. The gospel is working on us. Don't let your preparation time be simply about the content. Let the truths of God's Word soak in as you study. Let God work on your heart first, and then pray that He will change the hearts of the other people in your group.

THE
GOSPEL
PROJECT.

SESSION 1

WHEN FAITH
FAILS

"Faithless is he that says farewell when the road darkens." [1]

J. R. R. TOLKIEN (1892-1973)

INDIVIDUAL STUDY

Life is hard. Beyond the objective realities that we face in the world, such as disease, natural disasters, and death, there are other complications that happen along the way. Every day is filled with moments for decision-making. Some are simple, and some will change the course of your life forever.

Moments of decision come frequently in our lives, and the same was true of the people in the Bible. As we journey through the storyline of Scripture, we join the children of Israel as they come to the brink of the promised land for the first time. The God who promised to bring salvation to the world through the seed of Abraham has rescued Abraham's descendants from their slavery in Egypt. After a year in the wilderness, the Israelites have arrived at the doorstep to the land God promised. But before they enter, they are confronted with a decision that requires faith.

> When have you faced a decision that required faith? What helped or hindered your faith during that time?

In this session, we see how God is faithful, even when human faithlessness leads to tragedy. The Israelites failed the test of faith as they were called to enter the promised land. In their example, we see what happens when we start looking at our own strength instead of God's. When our faith fails, we forget the power God has demonstrated in the past and we lose sight of His future promise. When our faith fails, we need a faithful representative who will plead to God in our place. As you work through this session, ask the Spirit to examine your heart and grow your sense of gratitude for the greatness of God's faithfulness.

Throughout the week, engage these daily study sections on your own. Each of these examines different examples of humanity's faithlessness and God's faithfulness. There are three daily readings to prepare you before your group meets for this session. Interact with the Scriptures, and be ready to interact with your small group.

1 God's Strength, Not Ours

The Lord once said to Abraham that He would make a great people (the nation of Israel), send them into a great land (Canaan), and provide great blessings through them (see Gen. 12:1-3). Centuries later, the Lord was now ready to move this people into the land, but obstacles arose, tempting Israel to look at their own strength instead of God's.

> [1] The LORD spoke to Moses: [2] "Send men to scout out the land of Canaan I am giving to the Israelites. Send one man who is a leader among them from each of their ancestral tribes."
>
> ....
>
> [26] The men went back to Moses, Aaron, and the entire Israelite community in the Wilderness of Paran at Kadesh. They brought back a report for them and the whole community, and they showed them the fruit of the land. [27] They reported to Moses: "We went into the land where you sent us. Indeed it is flowing with milk and honey, and here is some of its fruit. [28] However, the people living in the land are strong, and the cities are large and fortified. We also saw the descendants of Anak there. [29] The Amalekites are living in the land of the Negev; the Hittites, Jebusites, and Amorites live in the hill country; and the Canaanites live by the sea and along the Jordan." [30] Then Caleb quieted the people in the presence of Moses and said, "We must go up and take possession of the land because we can certainly conquer it!" [31] But the men who had gone up with him responded, "We can't go up against the people because they are stronger than we are!" [32] So they gave a negative report to the Israelites about the land they had scouted: "The land we passed through to explore is one that devours its inhabitants, and all the people we saw in it are men of great size. [33] We even saw the Nephilim there—the descendants of Anak come from the Nephilim! To ourselves we seemed like grasshoppers, and we must have seemed the same to them."
>
> **NUMBERS 13:1-2,26-33**

Ordinary men weren't sent into the land to spy it out. Instead, God wanted leaders from each tribe to do the reconnaissance work. They would see what God was going to deliver and report back to the people. Then, acting on faith, the people could go forward to claim what God had promised.

The early part of the spies' report could be summarized like this: "It's better than you can possibly imagine!" The natural resources of the land were like nothing they'd seen before.

Having lived all of their lives in Egyptian slavery with a brief stint in the wilderness, such abundance was surely overwhelming. But as is often the case in the Old Testament, the Israelites faltered in their faith. Right on the heels of describing the land as everything they could hope for, the spies also described why it was impossible to possess.

> **Why was the land everything they could hope for? What were the obstacles to taking the land?**

Words like *large*, *strong*, and *fortified* were at the top of the spies' minds. When their faith faltered, they saw an unconquerable force before them. They took their eyes off the promise and put it on their enemies.

The spies had seen what they would have if the promise were fulfilled, but fear of the enemy caused them to lose faith. They had let go of their identity as the people of God. They were the people of promise, saved by the one true God, and commissioned to take the land God had for them. Instead, they looked at some really large soldiers and made a poor assessment of themselves, as if God were absent—"To ourselves we seemed like grasshoppers" (v. 33).

"Like grasshoppers" is how they described themselves, but it wasn't how the Lord would describe them. To God, the people were His children delivered from slavery and ready to take hold of the land of promise. This shows us that the failure of faith is both losing faith in God's power and losing a sense of yourself as a child in God's story of redemption.

Only through faith in God and His work do we gain a true understanding of the world and ourselves. Because of Christ's redemptive work on our behalf, our identity has changed. We're no longer an enemy, an outsider, a rebel, or lost in darkness. Instead, we're considered a member of God's family, an ambassador for Christ, and a child of light.

In the face of danger only Caleb and Joshua stood ready to forge ahead, but they were outnumbered by spies who believed the fortified cities were too great even for God to overcome.

> **When do you find it easiest for your feelings and fears to overwhelm your faith?**

2 God's Power and Promise

What's likely to happen when your faith begins to falter? In the Book of Numbers, we see a people that didn't reflect on what God had done in the past, neither did they look forward to God's future promise. They were overcome by fear of death and despair.

> [1] Then the whole community broke into loud cries, and the people wept that night. [2] All the Israelites complained about Moses and Aaron, and the whole community told them, "If only we had died in the land of Egypt, or if only we had died in this wilderness! [3] Why is the LORD bringing us into this land to die by the sword? Our wives and little children will become plunder. Wouldn't it be better for us to go back to Egypt?" [4] So they said to one another, "Let's appoint a leader and go back to Egypt." [5] Then Moses and Aaron fell down with their faces to the ground in front of the whole assembly of the Israelite community. [6] Joshua son of Nun and Caleb son of Jephunneh, who were among those who scouted out the land, tore their clothes [7] and said to the entire Israelite community: "The land we passed through and explored is an extremely good land. [8] If the LORD is pleased with us, He will bring us into this land, a land flowing with milk and honey, and give it to us. [9] Only don't rebel against the LORD, and don't be afraid of the people of the land, for we will devour them. Their protection has been removed from them, and the LORD is with us. Don't be afraid of them!" [10] While the whole community threatened to stone them, the glory of the LORD appeared to all the Israelites at the tent of meeting. [11] The LORD said to Moses, "How long will these people despise Me? How long will they not trust in Me despite all the signs I have performed among them? [12] I will strike them with a plague and destroy them. Then I will make you into a greater and mightier nation than they are."
>
> NUMBERS 14:1-12

When the leaders lost their faith, the people of Israel faced a crisis. Once the majority of spies said there was no hope, the Israelites went from wondering to mourning to outright rebellion. In the heat of the moment, the people's rebellion escalated. They took the ridiculous position that they would be better off dead! The people contemplated the merits of having died as slaves in Egypt or having died in the desert on the way to the promised land.

Moses and Aaron fell down in a posture of repentant prayer. Joshua and Caleb, the two faith-filled spies, tore their clothes as a sign of mourning. They entered into such postures because the rebellion of the people was a sin against God and grievous to the soul. These men wanted to lead their people toward faith in the God who fulfills His promises. Their slavery had been broken. Deliverance of the nation through the wilderness had been assured. The promised land they had awaited was within sight. This was all due to the gracious hand of God.

What do you turn to for strength in moments when your faith is faltering?

God's work in the past isn't only for the history books. It's the assurance of what He can do in your present circumstances. As the church, we must also look at our present circumstances from the viewpoint of God's work in the past and His promise for the future.

As believers, we have been freed from sin. The temptation we face is an impossible power to overcome—when we fight on our own. The Israelites faced enemies who were bigger, stronger, and had every perceivable advantage. The church stands against the world, the flesh, and the Devil, who all seem to carry an advantage over us, but this too is just perceived.

When have you faced a difficult circumstance from which God delivered you? Did reflecting on God's work in your life in the past give you strength to face that trial? Why or why not?

To ensure that the people clearly understood the gravity of both their history and their present circumstances, the Lord personally visited them. As Joshua and Caleb bowed down and cried out for the people to remember God's presence among them, God did the work Himself. Every work of God in our lives is an opportunity to trust Him more deeply.

As Christians, we have something the Israelites did not. We have the indwelling of the Holy Spirit. God personally resides in us, as believers in Jesus, to give a witness of His ongoing work. The Holy Spirit's presence with us is a down payment of what He has promised will be fulfilled in the future.

Why does the Spirit dwelling in us give us an advantage over the Israelites whenever our faith begins to falter?

③ Our Perfect Advocate

How did the Lord respond to the people's faithlessness in the Book of Numbers? He was ready to destroy them, until Moses began to intercede for his people. He lifted up the name of God and reminded God of His character:

> [13] But Moses replied to the LORD, "The Egyptians will hear about it, for by Your strength You brought up this people from them. [14] They will tell it to the inhabitants of this land. They have heard that You, LORD, are among these people, how You, LORD, are seen face to face, how Your cloud stands over them, and how You go before them in a pillar of cloud by day and in a pillar of fire by night. [15] If You kill this people with a single blow, the nations that have heard of Your fame will declare, [16] 'Since the LORD wasn't able to bring this people into the land He swore to give them, He has slaughtered them in the wilderness.' [17] "So now, may my LORD's power be magnified just as You have spoken: [18] The LORD is slow to anger and rich in faithful love, forgiving wrongdoing and rebellion. But He will not leave the guilty unpunished, bringing the consequences of the fathers' wrongdoing on the children to the third and fourth generation. [19] Please pardon the wrongdoing of this people, in keeping with the greatness of Your faithful love, just as You have forgiven them from Egypt until now." [20] The LORD responded, "I have pardoned them as you requested."
>
> **NUMBERS 14:13-20**

Moses stood before God as the representative for his people. He pleaded with God to show mercy so that the name of the Lord would be more widely known. Certainly, any work that God does proves His power, but Moses prayed that God would use this circumstance of the Hebrews' rebellion to display His power in His ability to forgive sin—once again.

Moses asked God to forgive "in keeping with the greatness of Your faithful love, just as You have forgiven them from Egypt until now" (v. 19). The forgiveness of our Heavenly Father is based on His love, not on our merit, penitent spirit, or ability to straighten out our lives. When God immediately pardoned the sin of the Israelites, He mentioned nothing of their ability to keep covenant faithfulness. The good news given to us by God is that His forgiveness is based on His power, not on our abilities.

What characteristics of God did Moses mention when pleading for mercy?

God could have displayed His power in judgment. Why do you think Moses asked for mercy?

When Moses stood before God and begged for mercy upon the people, he gave us a picture of what was to come. The people needed an advocate. They had one in Moses. The problem, however, was that Moses died, and he is still dead! This was a temporary advocacy by a temporary leader in a temporary time. We need a permanent solution.

God's pardon finds its ultimate fulfillment not in the temporary circumstance of the Israelites standing on the edge of the promised land. Rather, we have found it in the journey Jesus made to the cross, the grave, and rising from the dead. Only God in the flesh can be our perfect advocate.

Jesus lived as we do so as to sympathize with our weaknesses. Israel would spend 40 years in the wilderness, wandering around in faithlessness. Jesus spent 40 days in the wilderness being tempted by Satan, but unlike Israel, He passed the test. As the perfect representative, He gave the sacrifice we should give so as to grant salvation by His grace and through our faith. He rose from the dead, a state we can't overcome, so as to defeat sin, death, hell, and the Enemy. And now Jesus sits at the right hand of the Father to intercede for us every moment of our existence.

Furthermore, because we've been fully represented before God by Jesus, we now are able to represent God before the people of the world who don't know Him. Today, our calling isn't to conquer the nations but to take the gospel to them. No matter if the obstacles make us feel like "grasshoppers," we trust that God's power is greater than our own and that He will give us all we need to accomplish His mission.

As the people's representative, Moses showed interest in what "the nations" would think if God destroyed the Israelites. How can the church show interest in seeing that the glory of God's forgiveness is known among the nations?

GROUP STUDY

Warm Up

In life, do you tend to see obstacles or possibilities first? Explain.

When have you faced something that seemed impossible?

How did you approach the situation? What were the results?

When we consider what we face in life, we must view our circumstances in light of this reality: God has empowered believers to face both difficulties and temptations. God's Spirit works in us so that we can accomplish God's assignment for us.

During this time you will have an opportunity to discuss what God revealed to you throughout the week. Listed on the next page are some of the questions from your daily reading assignments. They will guide your small group discussion.

"For faith is only real when there is obedience, never without it, and faith only becomes faith in the act of obedience." [2]

DIETRICH BONHOEFFER (1906-1945)

Discussion

1. When have you faced a decision that required faith? What helped or hindered your faith during that time?

2. When do you find it easiest for your feelings and fears to overwhelm your faith?

3. What do you turn to for strength in moments when your faith is faltering? Why?

4. When have you faced a difficult circumstance from which God delivered you?

5. Did reflecting on God's work in your life in the past give you strength to face that trial? Why or why not?

6. Why does the Spirit dwelling in us give us an advantage over the Israelites whenever our faith begins to falter?

7. What characteristics of God did Moses mention when pleading for mercy?

8. How can the church show interest in seeing that the glory of God's forgiveness is known among the nations?

Conclusion

The world is filled with insurmountable obstacles. We face enemies stronger than we can imagine; our hearts fill up with doubts and fears that we try to fend off. But in the end, we need our Great High Priest, King Jesus, to rescue us from our sin, our fear, and our doubt. Just as God met the Hebrews in the desert with a desire to restore, He will meet you in the desert places of life. It's God's desire to redeem, not destroy. He enjoys delivering you into the work He has prepared for His people. It's the beauty of the gospel that leads us to repent and follow Him with a growing faith.

Spend some time praying this for you and for your group:

"God, we have seen Your sovereignty and faithfulness unfold throughout history. We know that nothing is impossible for You. Forgive us when we fail to trust Your plans. Strengthen our faith so that it will stand no matter what we face."

1. J.R.R. Tolkien, *The Fellowship of the Ring* (New York: Ballantine Books, 1982), 336.
2. Dietrich Bonhoeffer, *The Cost of Discipleship* (New York: Touchstone, 1995), 64
3. John Wesley, quoted in *Be Available*, by Warren Wiersbe (Colorado Springs: David C. Cook, 2010), 76.

"Give me a hundred men who fear nothing
but sin and love nothing but God,
and I will shake the gates of hell." [3]

JOHN WESLEY (1703-1791)

NOTES

SESSION 2

THE BRONZE SERPENT

"Whoever has been bitten by the snakes of sin
need only gaze on Christ and have
healing for the forgiveness of sins." [1]

AUGUSTINE (354-430)

INDIVIDUAL STUDY

At some point during my childhood, I was given a worry stone. I don't quite remember who gave it to me or why. But there it was in my junk drawer. It was a green, flat, teardrop-shaped stone that fit in the palm of my hand. In the center of its shape was an indention where the holder of the stone could rub his thumb against it. I didn't carry it often. But I do remember the sensation of moving my thumb back and forth across its smooth surface when I was nervous. It was the closest thing I had to a rabbit's foot or a four-leaf clover.

Throughout history, humans have demonstrated a tendency to collect trinkets we think will bring about good in our lives. It's the inherent need we have to stave off bad circumstances. We know that life isn't in our control, and we hope to find a way to convince the powers of the universe to be kind to us. As Christians, we don't believe in "luck," but we do believe in God's providence. By His power, He declares what's right, judges what's sin, and draws the rebellious back under His sovereignty. This was a lesson the Israelites needed often—as do we.

What are some items or activities people turn to for comfort?

What is the danger of depending on those things for relief or peace in our lives?

In this session, we see how during their time of wandering, the Israelites became ungrateful and impatient. As a consequence of their lack of reverence and trust, God sent poisonous snakes into their camp. In response to their pleas for mercy, God commanded Moses to lift a bronze serpent on a staff. Whenever someone looked at the serpent, they were healed. Jesus later claimed this story pointed forward to His being lifted high on the cross. By trusting in His identification with sinners, we're given eternal life and are called to be His ambassadors.

Throughout the week, engage these daily study sections on your own. We will examine the following truths as we look at the story of the bronze serpent: we deserve to be punished for our sin; God has rescued us from that punishment; we're called to share that hope with others. There are three daily readings to prepare you before your group meets for this session. Interact with the Scriptures, and be ready to interact with your small group.

① Punishment for Sin

The Israelite people had slavery behind them. But due to their unbelieving hearts, they had hardship before them. It was God's heart for them to enter into the land that flowed with milk and honey, but the Israelites were more likely to believe in the overwhelming circumstances of the moment rather than in the sovereign God who guided them.

In the next scene we explore, the Israelites are traveling toward the promised land in their 40th year of wandering. On the way, they have been provided with everything they needed. Yet, we will see how they spurned the Lord's provisions and affections by grumbling.

> 4 Then they set out from Mount Hor by way of the Red Sea to bypass the land of Edom, but the people became impatient because of the journey. 5 The people spoke against God and Moses: "Why have you led us up from Egypt to die in the wilderness? There is no bread or water, and we detest this wretched food!" 6 Then the LORD sent poisonous snakes among the people, and they bit them so that many Israelites died. 7 The people then came to Moses and said, "We have sinned by speaking against the LORD and against you. Intercede with the LORD so that He will take the snakes away from us." And Moses interceded for the people. 8 Then the LORD said to Moses, "Make a snake image and mount it on a pole. When anyone who is bitten looks at it, he will recover." 9 So Moses made a bronze snake and mounted it on a pole. Whenever someone was bitten, and he looked at the bronze snake, he recovered.
> NUMBERS 21:4-9

The people's rebellion shows up in a very simple word: impatient. The group of people who had been miraculously delivered, fed, and clothed by God now turned on Him. They went far beyond doubt. They accused God and Moses of treachery. They imagined God had intentionally led them out of Egypt for the express purpose of killing them in the desert. By stating such a claim, the people showed they doubted God's character and His word.

When have you allowed impatience with God's work in your life to cause you to grumble about what He has done?

What are some gifts we quickly take for granted?

In response to their rebellion, God acted quickly. He punished them. It was the type of punishment that would strike fear into the heart of any person. Suddenly, poisonous snakes were in the camp. Biting. Infecting. Killing. The break in their trust of God was a serious offense. The Lord didn't take it lightly. When they spoke out against their circumstances, they were speaking directly against God's character.

Modern-day readers may find it difficult to read about the punishment delivered against sin, but Scripture is clear: because God is committed to redeeming and restoring all things, sin must be punished and wiped out. Events like this remind us of the costly nature of sin. The Israelites had to once again learn that sin leads to death.

As the rebellious people began to die, they cried to Moses for help. The man whom they accused of being in league with a God who had deceived them would once again become their advocate. I wonder what Moses did. He may have shook his head, rolled his eyes, or simply sat down to weep over their continuous rebellion. But what we do know is that Moses was willing to plead the case of the guilty before the Lord.

Once God heard the people's penitent cry, He provided a way of restoration through their faith. In an act of divine irony, God instructed Moses to make a serpent of bronze and place it on a pole. If those bitten by the snakes on the ground would look to the snake that had been lifted up, they would be healed. The word for "looked" in Hebrew doesn't mean a casual gaze or a quick glance. Rather, it indicates fixing your gaze upon something or to look intently. The idea is that the Israelites would have to concentrate their mind's attention and heart's affection.

People in the camp listened to the Lord's word through Moses. As they suffered from poisonous injuries, they looked to the bronze serpent suspended in the air on a pole. As they gazed upon it intently, recovery occurred. Doubtless, it was a mystery to them. It's a mystery to us. God chose the symbol of their punishment for sin as the instrument of His mercy.

What's the significance of God's command to the people to gaze at the snake? What truths were the people to consider?

2 Christ's Rescue from Sin

The story of the Israelites' lack of faith, punishment, and recovery isn't one that stands on its own in biblical history. Jesus Himself referenced this story. In John 3, we read of Jesus' nighttime meeting with Nicodemus, a Pharisee and ruler of the Jews.

Jesus told Nicodemus that a person must be born again in order to enter the kingdom of God. Nicodemus was perplexed. What does being "born again" mean? Is it physical? Is it spiritual? What will it mean to a man who relies on his Jewish heritage? In answer to Nicodemus' question, Jesus pointed back through the annals of history to Numbers 21 and explained how the Son of Man must be lifted up just like the bronze serpent.

> 14 Just as Moses lifted up the snake in the wilderness, so the Son of Man must be lifted up, 15 so that everyone who believes in Him will have eternal life.
> JOHN 3:14-15

Packed into these two verses are several important ideas. First, we see how the original story is a foreshadowing of what Jesus would accomplish more than a thousand years later. When Moses lifted up the bronze serpent for the people to see, he was providing a remedy for all who would look at it. Now, Jesus is going to be lifted up for a much broader-reaching recovery. The bronze serpent's work was temporary; Jesus' work would be permanent.

Second, the word that is used in the Greek language for "lifted up" is not the pedestrian idea of simply holding something up to view. Rather, the Gospel writer employed a word that meant to exalt something. Just a few years after this encounter with Nicodemus, Jesus would be hanging on the cross. While there, He would fulfill the Old Testament prophecies of the divine Son of God, who is also fully human, serving as the payment for our sins. Christ would be exalted before the nations, and all who look to Him can live.

When you think about Jesus being lifted up on the cross, do you think of this primarily as humiliation or exaltation? Why?

How can it be both humiliation and exaltation at once?

Jesus' words to Nicodemus emphasized the centrality of His sacrifice. Unfortunately, the human tendency is to look to idols, not to the Savior.

Several centuries after the Numbers 21 episode, Hezekiah became king over Israel. He was a righteous king who destroyed the objects of idolatry in the kingdom. One item was the bronze serpent that Moses used in the desert. For all these years, the Israelites had kept it. At the time of Hezekiah taking the throne, "the Israelites burned incense to it" (2 Kings 18:4). The item that God used in one generation as His instrument of deliverance had become the object of worship in another generation. The people had forgotten God as the true deliverer and, as we are common to do, substituted an idol in His place.

Jesus, as He planned to go to the cross, would not become just one more "thing" for the history books. His body hanging upon the cross is not a relic for us to drag around or consider lightly. The bronze serpent offered temporary recovery. Everyone who was healed from the poison of the serpents still died eventually. Jesus was interested in a greater goal. John 3:15 tells us that everyone who believes in Jesus will gain eternal life.

"Everyone" is a powerful word. With it, there are no exceptions. Every single person who believes in Jesus is included in the promise that follows. There are no other requirements. Morality, vocation, economics, and influence hold no importance. Rather, every person who will believe will be given eternal life. It was probably a shocking thought to Nicodemus. In the cool of that night, he was confronted with the idea that eternal life could be granted to the faithful Jewish priest and the pagan Roman ruler. Jesus was offering salvation to everyone, and that was revolutionary for Nicodemus. It's likely revolutionary for all of us, too.

There's another perspective that we sometimes hold. It's about ourselves. We've met us. I get up in the morning and look in the mirror. What I see doesn't seem redeemable. It's not recoverable. After what I've done, is it possible that Jesus could include me in the "everyone"? The answer is a resounding *yes*. No matter your sin, your doubt, or your pain, God will grant you eternal life if you will look to the exalted Christ and believe.

> **Is it encouraging to you personally that everyone who believes in Jesus receives salvation? Why?**

3 The Foundation for Mission

Having entered into a faith-based relationship with Jesus, we now receive another great privilege. In Christ, we receive a new identity and a new role. We point others toward the Christ, and we say, "Look and live!"

> [20] Therefore, we are ambassadors for Christ, certain that God is appealing through us. We plead on Christ's behalf, "Be reconciled to God." [21] He made the One who did not know sin to be sin for us, so that we might become the righteousness of God in Him.
> 2 CORINTHIANS 5:20-21

Second Corinthians 5:21 can be understood better in light of Paul's teaching in other places on "imputation," that is, putting something in someone else's account. "Crediting" or "reckoning" or "accounting" something to another person is a biblical concept found as early as Genesis 15:6 and Psalm 32:1-3. God imputed sin to Jesus, and He imputes righteousness to sinners on the basis of faith.[2] By trusting in His identification with sinners, we're given eternal life and are called to be His ambassadors.

The apostle Paul wrote to the early church in Corinth to remind them of this role—ambassador. No longer the ancient Hebrew wanderers in a desert, they have become ambassadors for the King. It was a job that citizens of the teeming ancient city of Corinth would've understood well. Corinth was a coastal city positioned on a major trade route between Athens and Sparta. The city had emissaries from various political realms pass through on a regular basis.

An ambassador's role is straightforward. You represent a powerful ruler. The ambassador doesn't speak his own message but that of his king. He doesn't act on his own power but acts in the power of the kingdom where he is a citizen. Christians are called to this same work. We represent the King of glory, speak His message, and act on behalf of His kingdom. It's a right, a privilege, and a wonderful blessing.

> What is the relationship between Christ's becoming sin for us and our mission to plead with others to be reconciled to God (see verses 20-21)?

As ambassadors, we're called to share the message of salvation—a message that's both simple and profound. When someone believes in Jesus, they gain eternal life. That's the equation. It doesn't include a background check to see if they are worthy. A biblical knowledge quiz isn't administered to see how serious a person has been about church attendance. There are no litmus tests or additional steps required. It's a beautifully guaranteed answer to our darkest problem of sin. When Jesus says that He will do something, He does it. His nature of righteous integrity assures us that we can trust Him on it.

As Christ's ambassadors, our work is to plead with those who are outside of the kingdom to believe. We allow the Spirit of God to work through us to persuade the lost to find their hope in Christ. This is the place where the message of God and the mission of God come alive in the people of God. Whenever we say, "Be reconciled to God," to a lost person, it's an invitation for them to trust in the goodness of the King who has done all of the reconciling work on their behalf.

Paul taught that the One—our Savior Jesus—who is completely perfect became sin on our behalf. In order to pay for our sin, Jesus allowed Himself to be overtaken by the weight and judgment of sin. He does this seemingly impossible work so that you and I can be reconciled to God. By His work, an exchange is made. Jesus exchanged His goodness for our wretchedness. By our faith in Him, we exchange our sin for His righteousness. Neither party deserves what they receive, but we benefit by God's great work for us.

What does Christ's becoming sin for us communicate about God's character and love?

Because Christ has become sin for us, God calls us to plead with others to look upon the cross and receive spiritual healing. Whenever a Christian says to a friend or enemy, "Be reconciled to God," it's so much more than what they could imagine. We're inviting the lost to be found. The dying to be saved. The sinner to be made righteous by the very mercy of God.

GROUP STUDY

Warm Up

Would you consider yourself a patient person? What tests your patience the most?

Would you consider yourself a grateful person? When is the last time you expressed your gratitude to God? To others?

What happens when we allow impatience and ungratefulness to invade our lives?

Impatience and ungratefulness are powerful enemies to the life of joy we've been called to as children of God. We've seen this reality time and time again in the story of the Israelites. This session has been especially sobering as we've seen the consequences of their rebellion. But it has also been comforting as we've seen the infinite measure of God's grace.

During this time you will have an opportunity to discuss what God revealed to you throughout the week. Listed on the next page are some of the questions from your daily reading assignments. They will guide your small group discussion.

"Jesus became what was killing us—sin itself—when he was lifted up on the cross and thereby became the remedy for sin." [3]

NANCY GUTHRIE

Discussion

1. What are some items or activities people turn to for comfort?

2. What's the danger of depending on those things for relief or peace in our lives?

3. When have you allowed impatience with God's work in your life to cause you to grumble about what He has done?

4. What are some gifts we quickly take for granted?

5. When you think about Jesus being lifted up on the cross, do you think of this primarily as humiliation or exaltation? How can it be both humiliation and exaltation at once?

6. Is it encouraging to you personally that everyone who believes in Jesus receives salvation? Why?

7. What is the relationship between Christ's becoming sin for us and our mission to plead with others to be reconciled to God (see 2 Cor. 5:20-21)?

8. What does Christ's becoming sin for us communicate about God's character and love?

Conclusion

Jesus took on the weight of sin so that we who are sinners but sin could take on the glory of righteousness. The work that sin brings in our lives is a burden that requires God's eternal punishment. But Jesus has taken it all for us. His death in our place on the cross shows a love that's more than mere sentimentality. It's the decision to bear shame, undergo judgment, and pay all of the penalty.

With that thought, we're compelled by the love of Christ to work in His mission. He has done everything necessary for sinners to be cleansed. From the worst human being in history to the one we think the most moral—all need the salvation offered by Christ. As His people, we can and must declare it, live it, and converse about it at every turn.

Spend some time praying this for you and for your group:

"God, we are astounded at Your mercy and overwhelmed by Your grace. Thank You that the gift of salvation is available to everyone who believes in Jesus and the work He has done on our behalf. May our gratitude be shown by our love for Your mission. Compel us as Your ambassadors to speak the message of salvation everywhere we go to everyone we meet."

1. Augustine, Sermon 6.7, quoted in *John 1–10*, ed. Joel C. Elowsky, vol. IVa in *Ancient Christian Commentary on Scripture: New Testament* (Downers Grove: IVP, 2006), 124.
2. See "Impute, Imputation," by David S. Dockery, in *Holman Illustrated Bible Dictionary*, eds. Chad Brand, Charles Draper, and Archie England (Nashville: B&H, 2003), 812.
3. Nancy Guthrie, *The Lamb of God* (Wheaton: Crossway, 2012), 234.
4. Richard L. Pratt Jr., *I & II Corinthians, vol. 7* in *Holman New Testament Commentary* (Nashville: B&H, 2000), 360.

"[Paul's] practice was to tell others to be reconciled to God. Since Paul had to appeal to others to be reconciled, he did not believe that the work of Christ automatically reconciled every human being to God. Christ's saving work on the cross is sufficient for every human being, but it is effective only for those who believe." [4]

RICHARD L. PRATT JR.

NOTES

SESSION 3

THE GOD
WHO GOES
BEFORE

"Never be afraid to trust an unknown future to a known God." [1]

CORRIE TEN BOOM (1892-1983)

INDIVIDUAL STUDY

Military soldiers periodically practice drills from the early days of boot camp until the end of their career. Even though learning to march and following orders is mastered within the first few attempts, military leaders don't abandon the practice and simply assume soldiers will remember the basics. Drill is practiced because it teaches more than just muscle memory—it teaches obedience, discipline, and respect to generations to come by passing along the legacy. [2]

The Israelites had a legacy to pass along. God led their ancestors out of Egypt. He proved His ability to fight for His people and deliver them from a foreign territory. He demonstrated His sovereignty over the Pharaoh and nature's forces. He even proved His ability to go before the Israelites and make their paths straight.

In Egypt, God instructed the Israelites to prepare a Passover meal and to teach their children the meaning of the Passover throughout their generations (see Ex. 12:24-27). His instructions were akin to a military exercise because it taught future generations—through repetition and rehearsal—the value of obedience, discipline, and fear of the Lord their God.

> **What are some spiritual practices that we engage in to help "drill" the faith into us and pass it along to our children? How might these methods change over time?**

God spoke to Moses and gave him instructions for the Israelites before and during the Passover. Moses had spoken to God face to face (see Ex. 33:11) and was an integral part of life for Israel. But in Joshua 1, God made an announcement to Joshua that "Moses My servant is dead" (Josh. 1:2). For the first time in 40 years, the leadership position in Israel was vacant.

In this session, we see how God established Joshua as the new leader of His people. Many of the words and actions in Joshua 3 are reminiscent of God's previous words and actions in Israel's history. As we see how Israel was reminded to obey and revere God, trusting in His steadfast leadership, so we are inspired to trust in the God who goes before us.

Throughout the week, engage these daily study sections on your own. Each of these examines how and why we are to trust God with our lives and futures. There are three daily readings to prepare you before your group meets for this session. Interact with the Scriptures, and be ready to interact with your small group.

1 God Himself Goes Before Us

Joshua knew the people were prone to wander away from God. They suffered the consequences—God didn't allow the people who had seen His glory and signs in the exodus to enter the promised land (see Josh. 14:22-23). A generation later, God was ready to allow their descendants to cross into the land, and so He gave instructions to Joshua:

> 5 Joshua told the people, "Consecrate yourselves, because the LORD will do wonders among you tomorrow." 6 Then he said to the priests, "Take the ark of the covenant and go on ahead of the people." So they carried the ark of the covenant and went ahead of them. 7 The LORD spoke to Joshua: "Today I will begin to exalt you in the sight of all Israel, so they will know that I will be with you just as I was with Moses. 8 Command the priests carrying the ark of the covenant: When you reach the edge of the waters, stand in the Jordan." 9 Then Joshua told the Israelites, "Come closer and listen to the words of the LORD your God." 10 He said: "You will know that the living God is among you and that He will certainly dispossess before you the Canaanites, Hittites, Hivites, Perizzites, Girgashites, Amorites, and Jebusites 11 when the ark of the covenant of the Lord of all the earth goes ahead of you into the Jordan. 12 Now choose 12 men from the tribes of Israel, one man for each tribe. 13 When the feet of the priests who carry the ark of the LORD, the Lord of all the earth, come to rest in the Jordan's waters, its waters will be cut off. The water flowing downstream will stand up in a mass."
>
> JOSHUA 3:5-13

Joshua informed the people that God would perform mighty acts on the next day. The mighty acts weren't foretold; however, they were anticipated. It was the people's responsibility to prepare themselves for what God had prepared for them.

Preparation precedes divine production. Consecration, or purification, is an act of people setting themselves apart for the work of God in their midst. It's not just getting rid of outward distractions; it also includes wholeness of the heart, an inner preparation for God to move in and through us. The people needed to be ready for the miracles God would perform.

Why is it important to consecrate oneself and be spiritually prepared for God to work in mighty ways?

What are some examples of things we do to prepare our hearts?

The Lord reiterated His promise to Joshua and demonstrated that he was the new leader who was following the path of Moses. The Lord would be present with Joshua as He was with Moses and He would reveal Himself in similar ways. God went before Joshua and prepared the way. Joshua wouldn't have to vindicate himself or make himself respected among the Hebrew nation—God would exalt him in the sight of all Israel so they would have the same confidence in his leadership that they had in the leadership of Moses. Joshua's responsibility was to remain humble and trust that God would exalt him.

Why was it important for God to assure Joshua of His presence and power?

In what ways does God "go before us" in the struggles of our life?

God granted Joshua the authority to command the priests who were bearing the ark of the covenant to stand still in the Jordan. The waters, of course, would stop as soon as the soles of their feet touched the water's edge. The dry riverbed would be an additional miracle. The people would cross over into Canaan on dry ground.

This imperative, "Stand in the Jordan," reminds us of what God told Moses in Exodus 14:13 when the children of Israel stood at the edge of the Red Sea with Pharaoh in hot pursuit behind them. Moses said to the people, "Don't be afraid. Stand firm and see the LORD's salvation He will provide for you today" (Ex. 14:13). They stood still and God opened the Red Sea. Here the priests stood still in the midst of the Jordan River, which was soon to become an interstate highway for God's people to cross over into the promised land.

The people in this scene knew from their ancestors of God's power to part the waters, but now they would experience this miracle for themselves.

2 Obey in Faith

God publicly demonstrated His approval and support of Joshua as His chosen leader of Israel, so the Israelites could see that just as God had sanctioned Moses, He was now sanctioning Joshua. The people were to respond by respecting him as they had done with Moses. Their response would require faith—faith in God and faith in Joshua as their leader.

Now we arrive at the moment in which the people's faith was tested.

> ¹⁴ When the people broke camp to cross the Jordan, the priests carried the ark of the covenant ahead of the people. ¹⁵ Now the Jordan overflows its banks throughout the harvest season. But as soon as the priests carrying the ark reached the Jordan, their feet touched the water at its edge ¹⁶ and the water flowing downstream stood still, rising up in a mass that extended as far as Adam, a city next to Zarethan. The water flowing downstream into the Sea of the Arabah (the Dead Sea) was completely cut off, and the people crossed opposite Jericho. ¹⁷ The priests carrying the ark of the LORD's covenant stood firmly on dry ground in the middle of the Jordan, while all Israel crossed on dry ground until the entire nation had finished crossing the Jordan.
> JOSHUA 3:14-17

Imagine the scene as if you're one of the travelers walking toward the Jordan River with the others. Sure, you have heard the stories about the Israelites of old passing through the Red Sea on dry ground, but they're not here. This is largely a new generation of Israelites.

Perhaps you don't think the new generation has enough faith. Perhaps you don't believe your generation has worshiped enough. Perhaps you reflect on the laws and statutes that haven't been kept perfectly and you wonder if God will do for your generation what He did at the Red Sea. You continue walking—steadily stepping, steadily worrying, steadily having a conversation with yourself about faith or your lack thereof.

The priests make it to the edge of the Jordan. They step in and you see the waters to the north standing in a heap a good distance away. The waters to the south going toward the Dead Sea have been cut off. You blink. Can this be? The Jordan River is at flood stage (see Josh. 3:15), yet the land before you is dry. An interstate has opened for this generation. Can this be? Do you dare follow the ones walking in front of you? Can you trust your life to the crowd's actions? How tall can the water heap stand before it topples anyway?

How have you handled situations when you're more frightened by what lies ahead than confident your faith is strong?

Arthur John Gossip said, "William Shakespeare was correct in his perception that 'it is not difficult to bear other people's toothache; but when your own jaw is throbbing, that is another matter.'"[3] It's like that with faith. It's easy for believers to counsel others just to have faith. It's more difficult to face a personal crisis and offer the same advice.

This chapter is a vivid picture of the necessity of following God and doing things God's way in order to inherit God's blessings. John H. Sammis poetically expressed this truth in a hymn based on a young man's decision to follow God in faith. In response to D. L. Moody's sermon, the young man admitted to not understanding it all but having decided to follow God. Sammis wrote, "When we walk with the Lord in the light of His Word, what a glory He sheds on our way! While we do His good will, He abides with us still, and with all who will Trust and obey. Trust and obey, for there is no other way to be happy in Jesus, but to trust and obey."[4]

It's easy for believers to counsel others just to have faith. It's more difficult to face a personal crisis and offer the same advice. Israel lived in community with one another and could draw on one another for strength and encouragement in their struggles with obedience. God expected Israel to obey Him just as He expects Christians to obey Him.

How well is our church doing when it comes to supporting and encouraging one another to obey God in faith?

How can we do better?

3 Remember and Testify to His Power

Just as military drills are meant to foster obedience, discipline, and respect in generations to come by passing along the legacy through repetition and remembrance, lives of faith in Christ are meant to foster obedience, discipline, and respect in others through example and remembrance. The narrator in the Book of Joshua demonstrated the value of memorials and examples in Joshua 4:19-24.

> [19] The people came up from the Jordan on the tenth day of the first month, and camped at Gilgal on the eastern limits of Jericho. [20] Then Joshua set up in Gilgal the 12 stones they had taken from the Jordan, [21] and he said to the Israelites, "In the future, when your children ask their fathers, 'What is the meaning of these stones?' [22] you should tell your children, 'Israel crossed the Jordan on dry ground.' [23] For the LORD your God dried up the waters of the Jordan before you until you had crossed over, just as the LORD your God did to the Red Sea, which He dried up before us until we had crossed over. [24] This is so that all the people of the earth may know that the LORD's hand is mighty, and so that you may always fear the LORD your God."
>
> JOSHUA 4:19-24

Joshua commanded the 12 men representing the 12 tribes of Israel to bring stones from the middle of the Jordan. Those 12 stones were to be a memorial at Gilgal for future generations. The memorial stones that came from the place the priests stood while Israel crossed the Jordan would remind Israel of what God could do.

Why is it important for us to remember what God has done in the past?

Joshua revealed the reason for the stones that were taken out of the Jordan and set up at Gilgal. He anticipated the children of future generations would ask, "What do these stones mean?" Joshua made it obligatory for parents and leaders to tell the children of their generation that the stones were memorials and reminders that God had made a way through the Jordan River for Israel to pass over on dry ground.

Just as Joshua set up stones and told the Israelites how to respond when their children asked about their meaning (see Josh. 4:20-24), Moses told the Israelites what to teach their children in response to their questions at Passover (Ex. 13:14): "In the future, when your son asks you, 'What does this mean?' say to him, 'By the strength of His hand the LORD brought us out of Egypt, out of the place of slavery.'"

The stones had a story to tell. This is an indication of the obligation that parents have to disseminate the story of God in the history of the Jewish people as expressed in Deuteronomy 6:7: "Repeat them to your children. Talk about them when you sit in your house and when you walk along the road, when you lie down and when you get up."

These miracles took place in order to give testimony to all the people of the earth that God is almighty and He is to be feared and reverenced forever. Just as the stones had a story to tell, you and I have a story to tell.

> When was the last time you were able to give a testimony to God's powerful work in your life?

> How can we find strength in the testimony of others?

God calls us to remember and to testify of His power. God told Moses that miracles would happen "so [the Israelites] will believe that Yahweh, the God of their fathers, the God of Abraham, the God of Isaac, and the God of Jacob, has appeared to you" (Ex. 4:5). God calls us to tell the story of God's mighty works to one another and to unbelievers so they might believe.

> What kinds of thoughts, feelings, and fears inhibit you from sharing your testimony?

> What are some ways we can help each other overcome our reticence to testify to God's power?

GROUP STUDY

Warm Up

When was the last time you explored a place you'd never been?

What's the role of a guide? What benefit comes with having someone go before you who knows the way?

If you were to explore unfamiliar territory where safety is a concern, how important would it be to have a guide of some kind?

A guide is able to help us avoid dangerous situations in unfamiliar territory and can navigate us through difficult terrain. This is a picture of what it means to have someone go before us in a physical sense. From a spiritual standpoint, it's essential for us to recognize that God goes before us in every situation. Because God is present and powerful, we can trust in Him to guide us into the future that's unknown to us but known to Him.

During this time you will have an opportunity to discuss what God revealed to you throughout the week. Listed on the next page are some of the questions from your daily reading assignments. They will guide your small group discussion.

"As we prepare our hearts, souls, and minds for God to work, we position ourselves to expect Him, to hear Him, to see Him." [5]

MICHAEL CATT

Discussion

1. What are some spiritual practices that we engage in to help "drill" the faith into us and pass it along to our children? How might these methods change over time?

2. Why is it important to consecrate oneself and be spiritually prepared for God to work in mighty ways?

3. What are some examples of things we do to prepare our hearts?

4. In what ways does God "go before us" in the struggles of our life?

5. How well is our church doing when it comes to supporting and encouraging one another to obey God in faith? How can we do better?

6. When was the last time you were able to give a testimony to God's powerful work in your life?

7. What kinds of thoughts, feelings, and fears inhibit you from sharing your testimony?

8. How can we find strength in the testimony of others?

Conclusion

God told Joshua and the Israelites to set up memorial stones to remember what God had done to bring them into the promised land. Fast forward many generations to the last night Jesus spent with His disciples. He told them to remember the sacrifice He was going to make to save humanity from our sins. When Christians eat the Lord's Supper today, we remember God's plan to destroy sin through Jesus' death and resurrection.

It seems easy to take the Lord's Supper and miss the seriousness of the cross. There on the cross of Calvary, Jesus suffered alone. He who knew no sin became sin to redeem sinners. With blood dripping from His brow, His hands, and His feet as He died on the cross for sinners, He demonstrated His great love with His willingness to give His life on the cross for those who could never pay the price.

Don't ever forget the cross. God's miracles aren't simply for personal edification—they're meant to inspire those who learn about them to believe and give glory to God. He can give you the courage necessary to testify of Him.

Spend some time praying this for you and for your group:

"God, we're in awe of the mighty works You've done throughout history. Thank You for displaying Your power and authority over all things through miracles and wonders. Thank You, most of all, for the miracle of salvation made possible by the death and resurrection of Jesus. May we boast only in the cross and in Your redemptive power."

1. Corrie ten Boom, quoted in *Do Hard Things*, by Alex and Brett Harris (Colorado Springs: Multnomah, 2013) [eBook].
2. Anthony R. Mayne, "U.S. Army drill and ceremony provides discipline, esprit de corps for more than 238 years," U.S. Army [online], 27 June 2013 [cited 17 June 2015]. Available from the Internet: *army.mil*.
3. Arthur John Gossip, "When Life Tumbles In, What Then?" cited in *The Hero in Thy Soul: Being an Attempt to Face Life Gallantly* (New York: Charles Scribner's Sons, 1929), 109.
4. Robert J. Morgan, *Then Sings My Soul* (Nashville: Thomas Nelson, 2003), 220-21.
5. Michael Catt, *The Power of Surrender* (Nashville: B&H, 2010), 27.
6. Billy Graham, in *Billy Graham in Quotes*, eds. Franklin Graham with Donna Lee Toney (Nashville: Thomas Nelson, 2011), 136.

"Your faith may be just a little thread. It may be small and weak, but act on that faith. It does not matter how big your faith is, but rather, where your faith is." [6]

BILLY GRAHAM

NOTES

SESSION 4

THE GOD OF UNUSUAL VICTORIES

"Faith is to believe what you do not see; the reward
of this faith is to see what you believe."[1]

AUGUSTINE (354-430)

INDIVIDUAL STUDY

Wimbledon 2001 was the scene of one of the greatest dramatic events in tennis—it was, at least, for Goran Ivanisevic. The former 1992 Australian Open champion had fallen so far from his glory days that he needed the gift of a wild card to enter the Wimbledon tournament. He and the other players probably thought his presence wouldn't be much more than an uninteresting rerun. He had made it to three previous Wimbledon finals and was the lucky loser all three times. But this year was different, even though the final included a formidable opponent, double faults, superstition, and doubt. Against all odds, the 125th seeded wild card triumphantly held up the Wimbledon trophy. It was an unusual victory.

Joshua 6 contains one of the most dramatic scenes in all of Scripture. There is the protagonist—Israel; the antagonist—the city of Jericho; suspense—the marching around the wall of Jericho once a day for six days and seven times on the seventh day; and there's resolution—the wall of Jericho came tumbling down! Like Ivanisevic's win many years later, Israel's dramatic victory was against all odds. The Lord is the God of unusual victories.

> **What obstacles do people in our churches sometimes see as insurmountable?**

> **When have you been surprised by God's work in the past?**

In this session, we'll read the story of the fall of Jericho. The Israelites were commanded to obey God and follow His unusual instructions in the face of unfavorable odds. We'll see how God used apparent foolishness to confound the worldly wise. We'll see the power of an unseen God over visible might. And in the story of Rahab, we see God extending mercy and grace to anyone who will trust in Him. As believers in Christ, we trust God to fulfill His promises and extend mercy, and for this reason, we obey—even when the circumstances appear unusual.

Throughout the week, engage these daily study sections on your own. Each of these highlights God's power and victory over every enemy. There are three daily readings to prepare you before your group meets for this session. Interact with the Scriptures, and be ready to interact with your small group.

Victory Over His Enemies

At the start of Joshua 6, we know that God has promised victory in the promised land. But the plan He's about to reveal has no logical rationale. It offers no assurance of a military conquest. It has nothing to do with military might, and it doesn't include common weapons of warfare.

> [1] Now Jericho was strongly fortified because of the Israelites—no one leaving or entering. [2] The LORD said to Joshua, "Look, I have handed Jericho, its king, and its fighting men over to you. [3] March around the city with all the men of war, circling the city one time. Do this for six days. [4] Have seven priests carry seven ram's-horn trumpets in front of the ark. But on the seventh day, march around the city seven times, while the priests blow the trumpets. [5] When there is a prolonged blast of the horn and you hear its sound, have all the people give a mighty shout. Then the city wall will collapse, and the people will advance, each man straight ahead."
>
> JOSHUA 6:1-5

The city of Jericho was locked down. Its gates were tightly shut up because the inhabitants were fearful of Joshua and the Israelites. No citizen of Jericho was allowed to exit the city, and the king of Jericho and his army were trying vigilantly to prevent the Israelites from entering the city.

In chapter 2, the narrator allowed us to hear the words of Rahab the prostitute, who told the spies, "When we heard this, we lost heart, and everyone's courage failed because of you, for the LORD your God is God in heaven above and on earth below" (Josh. 2:11). The God who fights for Israel has a master key to every door in the universe and can open doors that are closed (see Rev. 3:7)—even those in Jericho. That's why, here, we see the Lord reiterating what He said generally in Joshua 1:3: "I have given you every place where the sole of your foot treads, just as I promised Moses."

But what a strange battle plan! How could marching around the wall of Jericho one time for six days and seven times on the seventh day ever bring down the massive wall that was wide enough, according to the ancient historian Josephus, for two chariots to ride on it side by side without falling over? Can you imagine the priests as they listened to Joshua give God's instructions? They probably wondered if Joshua was hearing God as well as Moses had heard Him. Surely Joshua missed a portion of God's instructions!

When God leads you in a specific direction, how do you hold fast to His instructions when others doubt whether or not you have heard from Him?

How do you weigh what you believe God is calling you to do with the doubts or concerns you hear from other people?

God gave Joshua a military formation that seemed to make them an easy target for Jericho. Military personnel comprised the vanguard. Directly behind them were seven priests who would blow the shofar. Positioned behind these seven priests were priests carrying the ark of the covenant (representing the presence of God in the midst of His people). The rearguard was stationed behind those priests. This assemblage was to march around the Jericho wall one time every day for six days and seven times on the seventh day.

God used a seemingly foolish battle plan to accomplish His purpose. But throughout this action plan, we see that the Israelites must be involved. God would execute what the Israelites implemented. God's people must participate in the battle of Jericho by marching around the wall and God would give them victory by bringing down the wall.

God told Joshua the priests would make an extended blowing of the shofar, which would be followed by the shouting of the entire army. God's unconventional battle plan showcased trumpet blowing preceding shouts, and the action would begin with a few and then spread to the rest of the people. Consequently, Jericho would experience an unimaginable cataclysmic and catastrophic event—the wall would collapse. God's plan, however, required the Israelites to act in faith.

How do your actions show belief in God's divine plan for your life?

2 Victory by Obeying

Joshua delivered God's marching orders, and the people prepared for victory by obeying. So they marched around the city once a day for six days. Can you imagine the questions and concerns going on in the minds of the Israelites as they began their first march? Regardless of any inward doubt, the Israelites obeyed God.

When life's realities make you weary, how do you ensure your thoughts and words point to faith in Christ (see 2 Cor. 10:5; Prov. 18:21)?

What are some ways believers can remind one another to focus on and obey God's plans instead of focusing on themselves and what others think?

Then came the moment of truth. The final day. The final instructions:

> [15] Early on the seventh day, they started at dawn and marched around the city seven times in the same way. That was the only day they marched around the city seven times. [16] After the seventh time, the priests blew the trumpets, and Joshua said to the people, "Shout! For the LORD has given you the city. [17] But the city and everything in it are set apart to the LORD for destruction. Only Rahab the prostitute and everyone with her in the house will live, because she hid the men we sent. [18] But keep yourselves from the things set apart, or you will be set apart for destruction. If you take any of those things, you will set apart the camp of Israel for destruction and bring disaster on it. [19] For all the silver and gold, and the articles of bronze and iron, are dedicated to the LORD and must go into the LORD's treasury." [20] So the people shouted, and the trumpets sounded. When they heard the blast of the trumpet, the people gave a great shout, and the wall collapsed. The people advanced into the city, each man straight ahead, and they captured the city. [21] They completely destroyed everything in the city with the sword—every man and woman, both young and old, and every ox, sheep, and donkey.
>
> JOSHUA 6:15-21

On the seventh day, the marching constituency made seven revolutions around the wall of Jericho. Marching around the wall seven times is significant. Seven is God's number of completeness. He created the earth and rested on the seventh day. Animals had to be seven days old before being used as a sacrifice (see Ex. 22:30). There are seven stems on the tabernacle's menorah, or lampstand. Seven is associated with God's judgment as well. There are seven woes to religious leaders in Matthew 23. There are seven seals of judgment, seven trumpets of judgment, and seven bowls of judgment in the Book of Revelation.

At the end of the seventh circuit around the wall, Joshua gave the command. The people shouted before the wall fell—not after. They shouted in faith, believing God had given them the city. Believers must not wait until the battle is over or until the wall has fallen—they must shout in their current situation, believing God will do everything He has promised.

God's instructions to the Israelites reveal the importance of words and actions. The people couldn't utter a word until Joshua gave the order to shout at the sound of the long trumpet blast. Perhaps God wanted the Israelites to display their faith in action before using voices to illustrate a lesson.

> **What are some ways we display our faith "in action" and how does faith "in action" give added credibility to expressing our faith "in words"?**

This story reveals how God works His victories through human obedience—the army marched, seven selected priests blew the shofar, and the masses shouted—it was only then that the wall fall. Faith produces works. Individuals involved in the march are obedient to God, walk by faith, and watch God do what only God can do—bring down the walls!

> **Why do you think God chooses to work through our obedience rather than apart from us?**

> **What does this teach us about our relationship to God?**

3 A Remnant Among His Enemies

This conquest of Jericho is a spectacular example of God's power exercised on behalf of His people and righteous judgment exercised on God's enemies. But it also contains a thread of mercy. As the conquest began, Joshua remembered the oath that the two spies had made with Rahab, who had given them shelter.

> [22] Joshua said to the two men who had scouted the land, "Go to the prostitute's house and bring the woman out of there, and all who are with her, just as you promised her." [23] So the young men who had scouted went in and brought out Rahab and her father, mother, brothers, and all who belonged to her. They brought out her whole family and settled them outside the camp of Israel. [24] They burned up the city and everything in it, but they put the silver and gold and the articles of bronze and iron into the treasury of the LORD's house. [25] However, Joshua spared Rahab the prostitute, her father's household, and all who belonged to her, because she hid the men Joshua had sent to spy on Jericho, and she lives in Israel to this day.
>
> JOSHUA 6:22-25

When Rahab is mentioned in Scripture, she often receives an infamous designation. She's called Rahab "the prostitute." In Joshua 2:1, the two spies entered Jericho and gathered at the house of "a prostitute named Rahab." In 6:17, her name is mentioned again with that same designation. In the passage above, the two spies were told by Joshua to go to "the prostitute's house." In Hebrews 11:31, the writer says that by faith "Rahab the prostitute" welcomed the spies and didn't perish with those (the king and people of Jericho) who were disobedient. James 2:25 refers to "Rahab the prostitute" as someone whose faith was demonstrated in works.

Interestingly enough, it's only when Rahab is associated with Jesus in His genealogy in Matthew 1:5 that this dubious designation is dropped. There, the text says, "Salmon fathered Boaz by Rahab" (not Rahab "the prostitute"). Boaz would marry Ruth, and they had a son named Obed. Obed had a son named Jesse. Jesse had a son named David, and Jesus is the descendant of David (also called the Son of David), which makes Rahab a great, great, great (you get the idea) grandmother of the Messiah.

What is the significance of Jesus having a woman in His ancestry who was once a prostitute?

How is God's grace to the undeserving on display in this story?

Despite her sordid past, Rahab was an effective witness. Compare her to Noah, for example. Noah spent decades telling his relatives they should come into the ark because it was going to rain. Only seven positively responded and were saved during the flood because they came into the ark—Noah's wife, his three sons and their wives.

But Rahab, in just a few weeks, accomplished the same feat. She brought her father, mother, brothers, and all her extended family members into the house. Because they were in the house with the scarlet cord in the window, they were spared.

What an amazing example of God's mercy! Like Rahab, believers are called to share the good news with unbelievers. We're to call people "into the house," letting them know they can be spared from the judgment of God through the blood of Jesus if they come inside. God spared Rahab and her family among the Israelites. They were preserved for a divine purpose.

Later, the prophet Zechariah would speak of a remnant from the enemies of God who would come to worship the Lord (see Zech. 14:16). Like Rahab and her family, the remnant would learn to worship God according to His will and His ways.

Make no mistake. Just as God kept His promise to the Israelites in the conquest of Jericho, God will keep His promise in preserving a remnant. For this reason, we trust God and obey Him by loving the enemies of God and praying for them to become followers of Christ. We reach out and teach through prayer, through the Word of God, and through our testimony.

It's easy for Christians to adopt an "us" versus "them" mentality with the world. How does God's promise to save people—even among His enemies—change our mind-set?

Describe a time when you were able to share this message of hope with someone who responded to the gospel.

GROUP STUDY

Warm Up

Do you remember the 1984 version of the movie *The Karate Kid*? Mr. Miyagi uses unconventional methods to train young Daniel in the art of karate.

> What were a few of the strange instructions Mr. Miyagi gave Daniel during their times together for training?

> How did Daniel respond and what caused him to question those methods?

> Have you ever received advice or instructions that seemed strange at first but worked in the end?

We pick up our story of the Israelites with an event that seems bizarre at first glance. God gives instructions for the attack on Jericho that go against any known military strategy. The plan even goes against common sense. God does this to showcase His power and authority and to compel His people to obey in faith.

During this time you will have an opportunity to discuss what God revealed to you throughout the week. Listed on the next page are some of the questions from your daily reading assignments. They will guide your small group discussion.

> "Where the instability of doubt is present, Christ may also be there—but where Christ is, the instability of doubt may not remain, for the Christ who commands us to believe will also give to us the power to believe."[2]
>
> MATTHEW LEE ANDERSON

Discussion

1. What obstacles do people in our churches sometimes see as insurmountable?

2. When have you been surprised by God's work in the past?

3. When God leads you in a specific direction, how do you hold fast to His instructions when others doubt whether or not you have heard from God at all?

4. What are some ways we display our faith "in action"?

5. Why do you think God chooses to work through our obedience rather than apart from us?

6. What does this teach us about our relationship to God?

7. How is God's grace to the undeserving on display in Rahab's story?

8. It's easy for Christians to adopt an "us" versus "them" mentality with the world. How does God's promise to save people—even among His enemies—change our mind-set?

Conclusion

Jesus set the perfect example for us of what obedience in faith looks like. Jesus' life teaches us to obey, act justly, love faithfulness, walk humbly with God, and make disciples. God's ultimate victory over His enemies took place through the faithful obedience of His Son on the cross. This divine victory offers new life and freedom to all who believe.

Stepping out in obedience isn't always easy for us as believers. Serving and ministering to the enemies of our God will require a deep trust in His sovereign grace. As His Spirit works in us, we're empowered to accomplish everything God calls us to do. Through witnessing to others, prayer, and study of the Word, believers participate in God's unusual victories.

Spend some time praying this for you and for your group:

"God, thank You for the victorious work of Christ whose death and resurrection has given us life. We praise You for the powerful ways you reveal Your sovereignty and Your mercy in this world. Help us to step out in faith as You lead us to do extraordinary things for Your glory."

1. Augustine, quoted in "Augustine of Hippo," Christianity in View [online], 24 May 2013 [cited 1 July 2015]. Available from the Internet: *christianityinview.com*.
2. Matthew Lee Anderson, *The End of Our Exploring* (Chicago: Moody, 2013) [eBook].
3. C. H. Spurgeon, *According to Promise* (New York: Funk & Wagnalls, 1887), 54.

"Faith obliterates time, annihilates distance, and brings future things at once into its possession." [3]

CHARLES SPURGEON (1834-1892)

NOTES

THE
**GOSPEL
PROJECT.**

SESSION 5

TAINTED BY SIN

"Achan had sinned against God's explicit command. As a result, God allowed his countrymen to be defeated. This was a tangible lesson that one person's sin can affect everyone around him. So it is within the fellowship of believers." [1]

HENRY T. BLACKABY AND RICHARD BLACKABY

INDIVIDUAL STUDY

In *All I Really Need to Know I Learned in Kindergarten*, Robert Fulghum tells about the street he grew up on, a dead-end street that was clearly marked. Despite the signs, he would see drivers navigate the two-block street until encountering a third sign located in the cul-de-sac—the one reading, "DEAD END." Fulghum speculates why drivers took the chance to drive down the street as if the two warning signs at the head of it were inaccurate: "So you drive as far as you can, even when you can clearly read the sign. You want to think you are exempt, that it doesn't apply to you. But it does."[2]

Christians can be like that sometimes. We see warnings in Scripture about sin and its consequences, and yet we persist in thinking that maybe the warning doesn't apply to us. We think we can keep from sinning, even if we put ourselves in a position of temptation. Or we think that if we sin, we surely won't face the consequences. We can keep it hidden or contained. Somehow, we will be exempt.

> **What are some warning signs you may encounter before you make a bad choice in life?**

> **In what way does consideration of sin's consequences deter you from sin?**

In this session, we will study the story of Achan and Israel's battle with the city of Ai. The story of Achan gives us a powerful picture of how one man's sin can affect everyone around him. It shows us the terrible punishment for sin (death) and the high cost of being tainted by sin. It also points forward to the glorious hope of seeing that sin dealt with on the cross.

Throughout the week, engage these daily study sections on your own. Each of these examines the seriousness of sin and how it must be dealt with. There are three daily readings to prepare you before your group meets for this session. Interact with the Scriptures, and be ready to interact with your small group.

The Sin of One Man

In Joshua 6:27, we read: "And the LORD was with Joshua, and his fame spread throughout the land." But chapter 7 opens with a change-of-direction conjunction that indicates whatever happened before will now be different.

> ¹ The Israelites, however, were unfaithful regarding the things set apart for destruction. Achan son of Carmi, son of Zabdi, son of Zerah, of the tribe of Judah, took some of what was set apart, and the LORD's anger burned against the Israelites. ² Joshua sent men from Jericho to Ai, which is near Beth-aven, east of Bethel, and told them, "Go up and scout the land." So the men went up and scouted Ai. ³ After returning to Joshua they reported to him, "Don't send all the people, but send about 2,000 or 3,000 men to attack Ai. Since the people of Ai are so few, don't wear out all our people there." ⁴ So about 3,000 men went up there, but they fled from the men of Ai. ⁵ The men of Ai struck down about 36 of them and chased them from outside the gate to the quarries, striking them down on the descent. As a result, the people's hearts melted and became like water. ⁶ Then Joshua tore his clothes and fell before the ark of the LORD with his face to the ground until evening, as did the elders of Israel; they all put dust on their heads. ⁷ "Oh, Lord GOD," Joshua said, "why did You ever bring these people across the Jordan to hand us over to the Amorites for our destruction? If only we had been content to remain on the other side of the Jordan! ⁸ What can I say, Lord, now that Israel has turned its back and run from its enemies? ⁹ When the Canaanites and all who live in the land hear about this, they will surround us and wipe out our name from the earth. Then what will You do about Your great name?" ¹⁰ The LORD then said to Joshua, "Stand up! Why are you on the ground? ¹¹ Israel has sinned. They have violated My covenant that I appointed for them. They have taken some of what was set apart. They have stolen, deceived, and put the things with their own belongings. ¹² This is why the Israelites cannot stand against their enemies. They will turn their backs and run from their enemies, because they have been set apart for destruction. I will no longer be with you unless you remove from you what is set apart."
>
> JOSHUA 7:1-12

Joshua sent spies to the city of Ai, just as he sent two spies to collect intelligence on Jericho (see Josh. 2:1). The spies returned with a jubilant (and somewhat arrogant) recommendation. Joshua usually received his marching orders from the Lord. But this time, he quickly accepted the recommendation and deployed 3,000 men to fight against Ai. In a surprising turn of events, this small city put the Israelites on the run. Israel had forgotten that it wasn't their army who defeated the much larger city of Jericho—it was the Lord who fought for them. They lost this battle because the Lord was no longer fighting for them.

What aspects of God's goodness are you most likely to take for granted?

How can we encourage one another to remember our dependence upon God's power and provision in our lives?

The text says the Israelites' "hearts melted and became like water" (7:5). What a surprising reuse of a familiar phrase! In Jericho, Rahab had said that the hearts of her people melted and there was no spirit left in any of them because of their fear of the Israelite nation.

Joshua reacted to this shattering news by tearing his clothes and falling on his face before the ark of the Lord. The elders of Israel put dust on their heads. Torn clothes signified mourning and repentance. Dust indicated great shame. Joshua didn't know what egregious act had caused God to turn against Israel, but he recognized the signs of God's disapproval.

In his prayer to God, Joshua sounded a lot like Moses (see Ex. 32:12-13; Num. 14:13-16; Deut. 9:28), who was always concerned about God's reputation among the surrounding nations. Joshua knew that God hadn't brought the people into the promised land to abandon them. Joshua's knowledge of the God of his fathers led him to repentance.

The reason for Israel's defeat was the presence of rebellion in the camp. A man named Achan had sinned, and God associated Achan's individual sin with the entire community. God indicted the entire nation, and His anger was leveled against all Israel. Sin is destructive. The sins of individual believers affect the family, the church, and the community.

Why do you think God allowed all the people to suffer when just one man committed the offense?

The Penalty for Sin Is Death

As Achan confessed his sin, he described what he did wrong. The three actions (I saw, I coveted, I took) are similar to the description of worldliness in 1 John 2:16 as "the lust of the flesh," "the lust of the eyes," and "the pride in one's lifestyle."

> [19] So Joshua said to Achan, "My son, give glory to the LORD, the God of Israel, and make a confession to Him. I urge you, tell me what you have done. Don't hide anything from me." [20] Achan replied to Joshua, "It is true. I have sinned against the LORD, the God of Israel. This is what I did: [21] When I saw among the spoils a beautiful cloak from Babylon, 200 silver shekels, and a bar of gold weighing 50 shekels, I coveted them and took them. You can see for yourself. They are concealed in the ground inside my tent, with the money under the cloak." [22] So Joshua sent messengers who ran to the tent, and there was the cloak, concealed in his tent, with the money underneath. [23] They took the things from inside the tent, brought them to Joshua and all the Israelites, and spread them out in the LORD's presence. [24] Then Joshua and all Israel with him took Achan son of Zerah, the silver, the cloak, and the bar of gold, his sons and daughters, his ox, donkey, and sheep, his tent, and all that he had, and brought them up to the Valley of Achor. [25] Joshua said, "Why have you troubled us? Today the LORD will trouble you!" So all Israel stoned them to death. They burned their bodies, threw stones on them, [26] and raised over him a large pile of rocks that remains to this day. Then the LORD turned from His burning anger. Therefore that place is called the Valley of Achor to this day.
>
> JOSHUA 7:19-26

For Achan, the lust of the flesh was apparent when he "coveted" (Josh. 7:21); the lust of the eyes was apparent when he "saw…a beautiful cloak from Babylon, 200 silver shekels, and a bar of gold weighing 50 shekels" (v. 21); and his pride was apparent when he "coveted them and took them" (v. 21), knowing that he was violating God's law concerning devoted things that were to be deposited in the treasury of the Lord.

Achan hid these treasures inside his tent. It's possible that members of his family saw him hide the forbidden treasure. If they knew, they kept silent, allowing Achan to look innocent on the outside. The inside of his tent revealed otherwise. First Samuel 16:7 declares, "Man does not see what the LORD sees, for man sees what is visible, but the LORD sees the heart," and Psalm 51:6 states, "You desire integrity in the inner self."

What are some ways we can help each other bring our sin out into the open?

Joshua asked Achan, with Israel standing as waiting participants, "Why have you troubled us? Today the LORD will trouble you!" (Josh. 7:25). In 1 Chronicles 2:7, Achan is later identified as "Achar," the troubler. With this nickname, we see how Achan has, in effect, traded places with Rahab. Rahab the prostitute acted faithfully and became a believer. Achan the troubler acted unfaithfully and became an idolater.

Since all Israel was affected by Achan's sin, which resulted in the defeat of the nation and the loss of 36 lives, all Israel picked up stones to stone Achan and his family. The community took responsibility for ridding themselves of the accursed thing. They also burned them. When the fire reduced the bodies of Achan, his family, livestock and stolen valuables to ashes, a stone memorial of infamy was placed over him as a warning to those who would consider transgressing the Word of God.

The chapter ends with these words, "Then the LORD turned from His burning anger" (Josh. 7:26). As frightening as this scene may seem, it later gives rise to a promise. In Hosea 2:14-15, God promised to one day "make the Valley of Achor into a gateway of hope." This place where Achan brought trouble upon Israel and then suffered the penalty of death for his sin would one day be a doorway to hope, because though the wages of sin is death, the gift of God is eternal life (see Rom. 6:23).

Unlike Achan, who took sacred things, Jesus Christ came to give the unthinkable—His life for ours (see 2 Cor. 5:21). Achan died for his sin so that the Lord's anger would turn from Israel. Jesus died for our sin so that we—who, like Achan, were enemies of God—could be reconciled to Him.

What happens when we minimize the horrible consequences of our sin?

Why does sin deserve death?

③ Enemies Are Overcome

> [1] The LORD said to Joshua, "Do not be afraid or discouraged. Take the whole military force with you and go attack Ai. Look, I have handed over to you the king of Ai, his people, city, and land. [2] Treat Ai and its king as you did Jericho and its king; you may plunder its spoil and livestock for yourselves. Set an ambush behind the city."
>
> JOSHUA 8:1-2

Though Joshua had uncovered the sin in the camp, he didn't presume success on the battlefield. This time, he listened to the Lord about the number of soldiers who should fight against Ai. God instructed Joshua to take all the soldiers with him and go to Ai. (Apparently, Joshua didn't go out to fight with the soldiers during the first battle between Israel and Ai.)

The Lord told Joshua that he and Israel would have a second chance—this was the second time around for them as they faced Ai in battle. The Lord informed Joshua that Ai would suffer what Israel had suffered when there was sin in the camp—defeat.

Interestingly enough, although the Israelites weren't permitted to keep the spoils in their victory against Jericho, this time God permitted them to take valuables (including livestock) and employ them for personal use. Had Achan waited on the Lord instead of disobeying the Lord's command regarding the valuables of Jericho, he would have been able to take valuables from Ai.

In the garden of Eden, Adam and Eve sinned against God. Eve saw, desired, and took the forbidden thing. Then, they hid from the Lord. As believers, we face the choice of following God or disobeying Him. Every time we face sin and refuse to repent, we harden our hearts toward God. We run *from* Him and hide rather than run *to* Him and repent. The story of Achan reminds us of the terrible consequences of sin.

Achan had opportunities to repent. Each time he entered his tent, he knew of his stolen, hidden treasure. When Joshua instructed the people to consecrate themselves (see Josh. 7:13), Achan should have repented during the process of consecration. Even before Joshua isolated Achan's family, Achan could have repented. Instead, because he hid his sin, Israel suffered a terrible defeat, and Achan lost everything—his life, his possessions, and his family. Sin resulted in death, and only after sin was dealt with could Israel move forward in victory.

The story of Achan gives us a powerful picture of how one man's sin can affect everyone around him. It shows us the terrible punishment for sin (death) and how God's enemies are overcome. This story shows us the high cost of being tainted by sin and points forward to the glorious hope of seeing that sin dealt with on the cross.

Why is repentance necessary in order for restoration to occur?

After the sin in Israel was dealt with, God told Joshua not to be discouraged or afraid. What is the connection between hidden sin and discouragement? Or hidden sin and fear?

Richard S. Hess gives us good insight into this passage, "God's words 'do not be afraid or discouraged' recall His first charge to Joshua, where they set the stage for His promise of presence and for the miracles that followed (see 1:9). With 'the whole military force,' Israel would again be united (unlike 7:3) and thus their victory was more likely. As with the promise about Jericho (see 6:2), God's instructions to Joshua began with the promise that victory was already assured. As with Jericho (see 6:21), all the people of Ai were to be destroyed."[3]

In what ways was joy restored to Israel after the sin in the camp was dealt with?

When have you experienced a time where your joy was restored after repentance?

GROUP STUDY

Warm Up

What products have you come across that advertised amazing results but in reality didn't deliver or live up to their hype?

Why do you think people sometimes fall for false advertising or marketing schemes?

How is the appeal of sin similar to these marketing schemes and false advertisements?

We want to believe the hype behind products that promise to make us smarter, healthier, and richer. Sin makes similar promises—it toys with our desires and leaves us wondering if we're missing out on something amazing. It tempts our flesh to want what isn't ours and to chase after fleeting pleasures. But the cost is infinitely higher than advertised. We see an example of this reality in the story of Achan and the tragic consequences of his hidden sin.

During this time you will have an opportunity to discuss what God revealed to you throughout the week. Listed on the next page are some of the questions from your daily reading assignments. They will guide your small group discussion.

"Does it make sense to pray for guidance about the future if we are not obeying in the thing that lies before us today? How many momentous events in Scripture depended on one person's seemingly small act of obedience! Rest assured: Do what God tells you to do now, and, depend upon it, you will be shown what to do next." [4]

ELISABETH ELLIOT (1926-2015)

Discussion

1. What are some warning signs you may encounter before you make a bad choice in life?

2. In what way does consideration of sin's consequences deter you from sin?

3. What aspects of God's goodness to you are you most likely to take for granted?

4. How can we encourage one another to remember our dependence upon God's power and provision in our lives?

5. What are some ways we can help each other bring our sin out into the open?

6. Why does sin deserve death?

7. Why is repentance necessary in order for restoration to occur?

8. When have you experienced a time where your joy was restored after repentance?

Conclusion

Joshua's ancestor Abraham was called a friend of God because he believed God. To have faith means to have confidence in something or put your trust in someone. Abraham entrusted his life to God and had confidence in God's plan for his life.

Conversely, enemies of God are alienated from Him and are hostile in their minds because of their evil behavior (see Col. 1:21). They don't trust God or seek to follow His ways. Enemies of God live as though God's rules don't apply to them. They're wrong.

The wages for sin is death; this is bad news. The good news is Jesus received these wages in our place and gave us the free gift of God—eternal life. Christians have a responsibility to live as people who were once tainted by sin but who have been washed white as snow by the blood of Jesus.

Spend some time praying this for you and for your group:

"God, help us to recognize the seriousness of sin and its consequences.
Keep us steady in the midst of temptation; draw our hearts to You
in repentance when we fail. Compel us to pursue holiness and
to point the world around us to Your glory with our lives."

1. Henry T. Blackaby and Richard Blackaby, *Hearing God's Voice* (Nashville: B&H, 2002), 178.
2. Robert Fulghum, *All I Really Need to Know I Learned in Kindergarten*, 15th ed. (New York: Ballantine Books, 2003), 108.
3. Richard S. Hess, in *HCSB Study Bible* (Nashville: B&H, 2010), 353-54, n. 8:1; n. 8:2.
4. Elisabeth Elliot, *Quest for Love: True Stories of Passion and Purity* (Grand Rapids: Revell, 2002), 145.
5. C. S. Lewis, *Mere Christianity*, in *The Complete C. S. Lewis Signature Classics* (New York: HarperOne, 2002), 121.

"[To have faith in Christ] means, of course, trying to do all that He says. There would be no sense in saying you trusted a person if you would not take his advice. Thus if you have really handed yourself over to Him, it must follow that you are trying to obey Him. But trying in a new way, a less worried way. Not doing these things in order to be saved, but because He has begun to save you already. Not hoping to get to Heaven as a reward for your actions, but inevitably wanting to act in a certain way because a first faint gleam of Heaven is already inside you."[5]

C. S. LEWIS (1898-1963)

NOTES

SESSION 6

IN LIGHT OF GOD'S SALVATION

"When we ask people what they want in church instead of giving them what they were created to long for, we play into the very idolatry that church was created to dismantle." [1]

JAMES MACDONALD

INDIVIDUAL STUDY

The nursery rhyme "Five Little Monkeys" is popular in households with little children. Perhaps you know it. "Five little monkeys jumping on the bed. One fell off and bumped his head. Mama called the doctor and the doctor said, 'No more monkeys jumping on the bed!'"

While this little ditty teaches the principle of subtraction, it also teaches an important life lesson: learn from the mistakes of others. As we've seen in our study of the Old Testament Book of Joshua, the Israelites have had many opportunities to learn from the mistakes of their ancestors and peers. All too often, they've repeated those mistakes in an on-going cycle of sin.

"Purity of heart is to think one thing," said Søren Kierkegaard, the Danish philosopher and theologian.[2] Kierkegaard believed we shouldn't think one thing while at the same time entertaining contradictory thoughts or actions. As leader of the Israelites, Joshua exemplified this kind of wholehearted devotion, and at the end of his life, he once again called on his people to choose God.

What are some actions that contradict what people say they believe?

Why is it important for Christians to act in ways that line up with what we say we believe?

In this session, we will read the story of Israel's choice to worship Yahweh as their God. Joshua, their leader, was near the end of his life. As he read the book of the law and gave Israel a choice (worship God or worship idols), he called the people to remember God's faithfulness and live in light of His salvation. Like the Israelites, we too are called to live in light of God's salvation by worshiping God in sincerity and truth, by putting away our idols, and by following Him in obedience.

Throughout the week, engage these daily study sections on your own. Each of these examines different ways we are to respond to God as His people. There are three daily readings to prepare you before your group meets for this session. Interact with the Scriptures, and be ready to interact with your small group.

1 In Sincerity and Truth

As we come to the end of Joshua's life, let's look back and reflect on his journey. This was a man who was born a slave in Egypt, a warrior under Moses, followed Moses' instructions, and successfully led the fight against Amalek. God had chosen Joshua and was preparing him for his future role when He told Moses, "Write this down on a scroll as a reminder and recite it to Joshua: I will completely blot out the memory of Amalek under heaven" (Ex. 17:14).

Joshua was one of the men who entered the promised land and spied on Israel's enemies that God would drive out before them. Only Joshua and Caleb returned with a report aligned with God's promise. After a long life of faithfulness in leading Israel, Joshua called on the people to live in light of God's salvation:

> [14] "Therefore, fear the LORD and worship Him in sincerity and truth. Get rid of the gods your fathers worshiped beyond the Euphrates River and in Egypt, and worship Yahweh."
> **JOSHUA 24:14**

Can you imagine the Israelites as they listened to Joshua? They might have thought Joshua sounded just like Moses did at the end of his life. The seriousness of the moment couldn't be escaped. There was no one to succeed Joshua. If the Israelites thought they were in trouble when Moses died, they likely were quaking in the sand at the thought of Joshua passing off the scene—not having a leader lined up to guide them, intercede for them, or communicate with God on their behalf!

In his words to the Israelites, Joshua gave key instructions that got to the heart of worship—fear the Lord; worship, or serve, Him in sincerity and truth; and get rid of the gods of your fathers. Joshua's directives implored Israel to serve the God who had saved them. (The biblical understanding of servanthood has its foundation in people serving God in worship. The terms for "service" and "worship" are often interchangeable. [3])

What would you say are characteristics of worship done "in sincerity and truth"?

What characteristics would be found in insincere, untruthful worship?

Notice how Joshua addressed both positive and negative elements in serving the Lord. Positively, the Lord was to be served in sincerity, that is, without hypocrisy and in faithfulness. Negatively, the Lord was to be served by discarding their false gods, the idols the Israelites' ancestors had worshiped.

Joshua's instructions are applicable to believers today because God is unchangeable. He still equips those He calls but now believers are equipped by the indwelling of the Holy Spirit. As Ray Stedman stated: "The Christian is more than an empty vessel. He has something within—or, more accurately, Someone within. We have a treasure in our clay pot! And more than a treasure—a transcendent power! That is humanity as God intended it to be. The clay pot is not much in itself, but it holds an inestimable treasure, beyond price, and a transcendent power, greater than any other power known to humanity." [4]

Though our experiences occur in a different era, God's standard of holiness remains steadfast. Fearing God still means standing in awe of Him. It's easy to imagine standing in awe in the presence of your favorite athlete, scholar, or movie star. But just think about it—we're always in the presence of God (see Ps. 139:7-12) and should tremble at His displeasure.

For this reason, serving God, as Joshua instructed, must be done with integrity. The word for "sincerity" here is also used by David in Psalm 18:25, a psalm about God rescuing him from his enemies. In his song to the Lord, David said God repaid him (David, an upright man) with His uprightness. In Joshua's speech, his use of this strong word was intended to lead the Israelites to serve God wholeheartedly and to fear the cost of half-hearted devotion.

Joshua also instructed the congregation to worship God in truth. This is the opposite of pretending. Joshua's words were commands with a tinge of warning—be people of integrity. God knows our hearts and our inner thoughts.

How does God's salvation through Jesus Christ lead us to be in awe of Him?

What role does this sense of awe play in leading us to sincere and truthful worship?

2 Put Away Idols

As Joshua continued to instruct the Israelites, he acknowledged that serving the Lord isn't something that can be coerced. For our obedience to please the Lord, it must be given willingly. So, Joshua set before the people a choice.

> [15] But if it doesn't please you to worship Yahweh, choose for yourselves today the one you will worship: the gods your fathers worshiped beyond the Euphrates River or the gods of the Amorites in whose land you are living. As for me and my family, we will worship Yahweh." [16] The people replied, "We will certainly not abandon the LORD to worship other gods! [17] For the LORD our God brought us and our fathers out of the land of Egypt, out of the place of slavery, and performed these great signs before our eyes. He also protected us all along the way we went and among all the peoples whose lands we traveled through. [18] The LORD drove out before us all the peoples, including the Amorites who lived in the land. We too will worship the LORD, because He is our God." [19] But Joshua told the people, "You will not be able to worship Yahweh, because He is a holy God. He is a jealous God; He will not remove your transgressions and sins. [20] If you abandon the LORD and worship foreign gods, He will turn against you, harm you, and completely destroy you, after He has been good to you." [21] "No!" the people answered Joshua. "We will worship the LORD." [22] Joshua then told the people, "You are witnesses against yourselves that you yourselves have chosen to worship Yahweh." "We are witnesses," they said. [23] "Then get rid of the foreign gods that are among you and offer your hearts to the LORD, the God of Israel."
>
> JOSHUA 24:15-23

The Israelites understood the implications of Joshua's words as they listened to him. Joshua offered the Israelites a choice. If it seemed evil, or displeasing, for them to serve the Lord, then they could direct their allegiance to false deities that had already been proven powerless.

Joshua didn't offer them the luxury of neutrality—they couldn't serve the one true God of Israel and false gods. And then, in one of the great acknowledgments of an individual's undivided loyalty to God, Joshua affirmed that he and his house would serve the Lord.

What are some ways that a family can cultivate devotion to the Lord's service?

The people responded to Joshua with a congregational "Amen!" This was their verbal understanding that it would be ludicrous to forsake the Lord in order to serve false gods. This congregational commitment was based upon God's involvement in their history. They knew it was the Lord who worked wonders from generation to generation to keep His promise to Abraham (see Gen. 12).

But then Joshua made a surprising statement: "You will not be able to worship Yahweh, because He is a holy God. He is a jealous God" (Josh. 24:19). Was this a statement of judgment? Did Joshua set them up just to tear them down? No. Joshua realistically looked beyond their passionate declaration. He knew that Israel had often forgotten the God who had rescued them. He knew their sinful tendencies and their past unfaithfulness.

God is holy and jealous (see Ex. 20:5). For this reason, as Joshua stated, He wouldn't overlook their "transgressions" or "sins." *Transgression* means to break the covenant or go beyond the limits. *Sin* means to miss the mark or go the wrong way. God called out both sin and transgression as He identified Israel's wrongs in the story of Achan in Joshua 7:11.

Serving the Lord was a serious matter. It required more than an easy, verbal congregational resolution. Rejecting the Lord would bring serious consequences upon those who forsook Him to serve foreign gods. But in spite of Joshua's objection, the Israelites remained steady and once again made an affirmative confession.

We can understand their decision. They knew the fear of crossing the Jordan and felt the ground tremble as the wall of Jericho tumbled down. They knew the awesomeness of God's might displayed over and over as they possessed land they didn't own. In light of God's salvation, Joshua called the people to put away their idols and to set themselves as witnesses against themselves if they were to disobey.

How does Joshua's frank and honest assessment of Israel's inability to be faithful strike you?

In what way is our commitment to worship God in light of Christ's salvation different than the Israelites' commitment?

3 Commit to Obedience

As we come to the end of this section of Scripture, we see once again the people making a jubilant vow: "We will worship the LORD our God and obey Him" (Josh. 24:24). They remembered God's faithfulness and knew He had the power to deliver them.

> 24 So the people said to Joshua, "We will worship the LORD our God and obey Him." 25 On that day Joshua made a covenant for the people at Shechem and established a statute and ordinance for them. 26 Joshua recorded these things in the book of the law of God; he also took a large stone and set it up there under the oak next to the sanctuary of the LORD. 27 And Joshua said to all the people, "You see this stone—it will be a witness against us, for it has heard all the words the LORD said to us, and it will be a witness against you, so that you will not deny your God." 28 Then Joshua sent the people away, each to his own inheritance.
>
> JOSHUA 24:24-28

Joshua wanted the people to count the cost. He established a way to judge whether or not the Israelites were keeping the vow they made to the Lord—the statutes and rules from the Torah. These rules served as reminders of their obligation to live out their verbal confession. These rules provided the measure for their commitment to God.

What is the significance of Joshua erecting a physical stone to remind the people of their commitment?

What actions in our homes and churches help remind us of our calling to live in light of God's salvation?

Joshua made a covenant with the people, wrote these words in the book of the law of God, and took a large stone and personified it. The stone would serve as a witness, a visible prosecuting attorney against Israel if they didn't live out their confession of being faithful to God.

Richard Hess gives us more insight on the memorial Joshua built: "The stone served as a lasting memorial that would remind future generations of the covenant made at Shechem

and its importance. Jacob's connection with a stone and with Shechem is especially significant for this passage. At Shechem, Jacob buried all the foreign gods that his wives and
concubines brought from their family home in Haran (see Gen. 35:2-4). The erection of a
stone witness at this same spot confirms that the people don't intend to worship these deities.
However, it may also identify the place where the images were buried. Thus the ambiguity of
the place remains. Will Israel worship the Lord alone, as symbolized by the stone of witness,
or will it return to this spot in order to worship other deities, as symbolized by the buried
images? Israel's choice to betray its promise (see Judg. 2:11-13) was signaled by its omission
of any reference to foreign deities in response to Joshua's challenge (see Josh. 24:23-24). This
also contrasts with Jacob whose command to his family to put away their deities met with a
positive response (see Gen. 35:2-4)." [5]

Since the people seemed adamant about sincerely serving the Lord, Joshua dismissed the
congregation and permitted them to go back to their homes in their newly assigned territo-
ries. The Israelites would bear responsibility for their covenant with God without Joshua's
leadership because he would soon die.

The story of Joshua reminds us of the responsibility we have to disciple the next generation.
Parents have the responsibility of directing their children by training them in the way they
should go (see Prov. 22:6). We submit to the training of God through various circumstances
and seek to live in obedience, trusting Him to empower us to follow in His ways. God calls
us to put away our idols and display for the world a new way of living, made possible only
through Christ's salvation.

> **Why is it important that we see our obedience in light of God's salvation
> and not as a way of earning God's salvation?**

GROUP STUDY

Warm Up

What is your favorite worship song? Why?

How would you define worship? Why do you think some people equate worship with the music portion of a church service?

How is obedience an act of sincere worship?

We're called to worship God in sincerity and truth. Worship is our response to His grace and glory. When we recognize the Lord's faithfulness in our lives, we should respond in gratitude, in humble submission, and in sincere worship.

During this time you will have an opportunity to discuss what God revealed to you throughout the week. Listed on the next page are some of the questions from your daily reading assignments. They will guide your small group discussion.

"We are products of our past, but we don't have to be prisoners of it." [6]

RICK WARREN

Discussion

1. What are some actions that contradict what people say they believe?

2. Why is it important for Christians to act in ways that line up with what we say we believe?

3. What would you say are characteristics of worship done "in sincerity and truth"?

4. What characteristics would be found in insincere, untruthful worship?

5. How does God's salvation through Jesus Christ lead us to be in awe of Him? What role does this sense of awe play in leading us to sincere and truthful worship?

6. In what way is our commitment to worship God in light of Christ's salvation different than the Israelites' commitment?

7. What actions in our homes and churches help remind us of our calling to live in light of God's salvation?

8. Why is it important that we see our obedience in light of God's salvation and not as a way of earning God's salvation?

Conclusion

Like Joshua, believers must count the cost, considering the annals of time and the record of history to remember God's plan for good and not evil to those who believe (see Jer. 29:11). Joshua's faithfulness was rewarded and he was called "the LORD's servant" at the end of his life (see Josh. 24:29).

Also, like Joshua, we are to have a realistic understanding of our ability (or inability) to obey God perfectly. The beautiful difference between our situation and Israel's is that we have an even greater leader than Joshua—Jesus Christ, God's chosen servant who brings us not into the earthly promised land but into our eternal inheritance. The children of Israel were unable to keep their vows, but because we have the Holy Spirit living inside of us and guiding us, we are empowered to live in light of God's salvation and to point the world around us to that light.

Spend some time praying this for you and for your group:

"God, remind us of Your faithfulness throughout history and let our response to Your goodness be heartfelt worship and adoration. Teach us to praise You with sincere motives from the depths of our gratitude. Thank You for the gift of the Holy Spirit who enables us to honor You with our lives."

1. James MacDonald, *Vertical Church* (Colorado Springs: David Cook, 2012) [eBook].
2. Søren Kierkegaard, *Purity of Heart Is to Will One Thing* (New York City: Start Publishing, 2012).
3. Martin H. Manser, "Dictionary of Biblical Themes," Bible Hub [online], 2009 [cited 16 July 2015]. Available from the Internet: *biblehub.com*.
4. Ray C. Stedman, "Pots, Pressures and Power," Authentic Christianity [online], 1975 [cited 16 July 2015]. Available from the Internet: *raystedman.org*.
5. Richard S. Hess, Joshua, in *Tyndale Old Testament Commentaries* (Downers Grove: IVP, 1996), 174.
6. Rick Warren, *The Purpose Driven Life* (Grand Rapids: Zondervan, 2012) [eBook].
7. D. L. Moody, "The Way of Life," in *The D. L. Moody Collection* (Chicago: Moody, 1997), 313.

"May God help [us] to submit without
delay [our] proud will in loving,
child-like obedience to Himself." [7]

D. L. MOODY (1837-1899)

NOTES

SMALL-GROUP TIPS

Reading through this section and utilizing the suggested principles and practices will greatly enhance the group experience. First is to accept your limitations. You cannot transform a life. Your group must be devoted to the Bible, the Holy Spirit, and the power of Christian community. In doing so your group will have all the tools necessary to draw closer to God and to each other—and to experience heart transformation.

GENERAL TIPS:

- Prepare for each meeting by reviewing the material, praying for each group member, and asking the Holy Spirit to work through you as you point to Jesus each week.

- Make new attendees feel welcome.

- Think of ways to connect with group members away from group time. The amount of participation you have during your group meetings is directly related to the time you take to connect with your group members away from the group meeting. Consider sending emails, texts, or social networking messages encouraging members in their personal devotion times prior to the session.

MATERIALS NEEDED:

- Bible

- Bible study book

- Pen/pencil

PROVIDE RESOURCES FOR GUESTS:

- An inexpensive way to make first-time guests feel welcome is to provide them a copy of your Bible study book. Estimate how many first-time guests you can expect during the course of your study, and secure that number of books. What about people who have not yet visited your group? You can encourage them to visit by providing a copy of the Bible study book.

SMALL-GROUP VALUES

Meeting together to study God's Word and experience life together is an exciting adventure. Here are values to consider for small-group experiences:

COMMUNITY: God is relational, so He created us to live in relationship with Him and one another. Authentic community involves sharing life together and connecting on many levels with others in our group.

INTERACTIVE BIBLE STUDY: God gave the Bible as the testimony of His work in the world, which ultimately points to Jesus Christ. We need to deepen our understanding of God's Word. People learn and remember more as they wrestle with truth and learn from others. Bible discovery and group interaction will enhance spiritual growth.

EXPERIENTIAL GROWTH: Beyond solely reading, studying, and dissecting the Bible, being a disciple of Christ involves marrying knowledge and experience. We do this by taking questions to God, opening a dialogue with our hearts, and utilizing other ways to listen to God speak (other people, nature, circumstances, etc.). Experiential growth is always grounded in the Bible as God's primary revelation and our ultimate truth-source.

POWER OF GOD: Processes and strategies will be ineffective unless we invite and embrace the presence and power of God. In order to experience community and growth, Jesus needs to be the centerpiece of our group experiences, and the Holy Spirit must be at work.

REDEMPTIVE COMMUNITY: Healing best occurs within the context of community and relationships. It's vital to see ourselves through the eyes of others, share our stories, and ultimately find freedom from the secrets and lies that enslave our souls.

MISSION: God has invited us into a larger story with a great mission of setting captives free and healing the broken-hearted (see Isa. 61:1-2). However, we can only join in this mission to the degree that we've let Jesus bind up our wounds and set us free. Others will be attracted to an authentic, redemptive community.

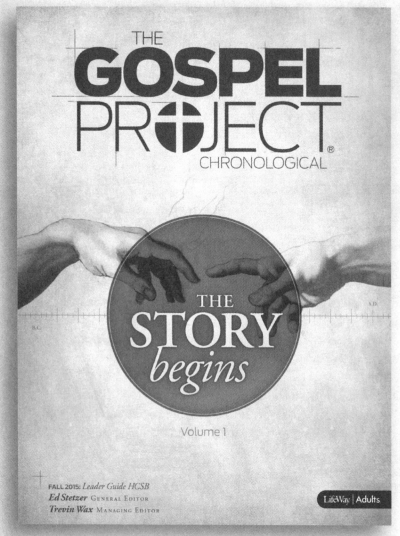